# A

# Book of

# "African"

# "American"

# Art

# By Ann Onimity

You may wonder why I used the pseudonym that is "Ann Onimity". If you are an etymologist you know that the two separate hold some ambiguity. But if you join the two you will get what you are looking for. The word anonymity is, at least the root of it, anonymous, is quite old. But, its meaning has held true throughout the ages. It brings to mind two lines from a poem I read once:

## I would rather touch the heart of a multitude
## Than do all that it takes to be famous

How apropos these words are for me. I want every person who reads these stories, even though they are fiction, to understand that these women really exist. And you may have the unique treasure of knowing one or a few of them. If you close your eyes and allow your heart to see, you will be able to find them. When you do love and cherish them as they deserve. This book is dedicated to all of them. Therefore when you read it understand that I am of the human race and that is all the color you need to worry about. I hope to meet you again one day. Please look for the continuation of most of the stories in my next foray. Thank you for your time and consideration. It is truly appreciated.

Ann

Contents:

# Prologue

I imagine that when you picked this book up you thought it was going to be a lot of pictures drawn, painted, or taken by black people. Or even pictures of black people.

This is another take on the word 'art'. I think that art is any form of expression that enlightens, enhances, or expounds on some part of the psyche.

That is what this is. I have decided to give voice to the thoughts of several African women from an American perspective. I have never met the women in my montage of tales, but all of them are me. All of them are just women trying to deal with what life has put before them. These are my words. These are your words. These are their words. Can't you hear them shouting?

# LISTEN

# An African American Woman

Why do you refer to me in such a way?
I don't hear you saying Caucasian woman
I don't hear you saying Asian, but anyway
I'll explain it as well as I can

Why can I not be of the human race?
The one of which we all belong
There are things in life that I must face
Why don't I explain, come along

I am a woman first no matter my color
And don't you misunderstand
I am strong, loving, caring, I HOLLAR!
Don't be afraid, give me your hand


I will not accept this category given
This African American Name
By heart and soul, not color, I am driven
And you should be the same


Take my words and commit them to heart
Live according to your thoughts
If you are kind, if you are smart
No matter your color, dignity you have
sought

This is for all the women who refuse
To be labeled African American
They will not hide, become recluse
They will stand out as strong women


Be who you are no matter your color
© 2003 B. Renee Williamson

# Her Kindness, My Injustice

"What are you doing there?" We rushed to her side as she lay there watching her baby boy futilely gasping, trying desperately to get air. "Why are you doing that, are you crazy?!" He was hardly moving. I knew that if we didn't do something quickly there would be no hope for the child.

I pushed her away from the infant and gently poked a hole, tearing the bag open. The boy took a stilted breath and started wailing.  It was the most glorious sound I had ever heard.

"What were you trying to do?"

I couldn't understand how someone would try to kill their own child.  This place is a place of peace and love.  That is something foreign here.  Now, back home in Philly there might be an occasion for this sort of thing.  That was part of the reason I came to Africa.  I wanted to see a different way of life.  I wanted to see where everyone says I came from.  It seems that life is the same no matter where you go.  It's horrific and wonderful all at the same time.

Tearfully she handed be a piece of rough paper with scrawled French writing on it and said, "Read this."  I took the single sheet from her and read it (in actuality one of the guides translated it for me.  I could speak coherent French, but I could barely read it.):

"All the things that have been happening are your fault. The animals are dying and the crops have all but died. You will have to go. When your husband was killed by that lion, we thought the kind thing would be to let you stay. And the baby that was born that day was a healthy boy we thought all the badness had gone out of your family's line. If it had been a girl we would have immediately put it to death. But a healthy boy is always an indication of good things.

But, not so long after that the animals started dying, again, we now see that we were mistaken. If you kill the child, it will demonstrate your desire to remove yourself from this awful situation your husband caused. You have the ability to redeem your father's house. It is apparent to us that you are fertile. Your father has suffered so many losses. First, the horrible loss, during the wars, of every one of his sons, and then his wife died in childbirth. What more can the man endure? By having a healthy boy even through the sickness that you had is a sign that you are able to produce strong, healthy boys to carry the tribe into the future.

So, the choice is yours. Either you rid the village of this curse that your husband brought into the village, by killing the child. Or you leave. If you don't leave or kill the child due to your feminine weakness we will kill you and the child and burn your hut!

"What else can I do? if I kill the child they will let me stay. They will think the curse ends with him."

"How can you know that?" I queried

She sighed and said, "My father is the one who is the curse. He only let me marry

Amadi because of his name, which means 'free man.' It also can mean 'seemed destined to die at birth.' The council of chiefs thought that this was a sign that the man was free of any defects. No one in our village would marry me because I was the only remaining of my father's children and they were afraid I would only produce girls."

As she was explaining a wayward thought entered my mind, "it is the man who chooses the sex of the baby through his genes, not the woman", but I really am not sure I should interrupt her story. Would she believe me anyway?.............

"When my mother died in childbirth and the child was discovered to be a girl, well that made it worse. Within months of getting married I was pregnant and when I gave birth to a healthy son, it was the happiest and the saddest day of my life. Because *when the lion killed my husband I saw it. When I began laboring to have the child the lion was near and smelled the blood and tried to kill me. We were on the way home from visiting his village. It is through the wood over that way. My husband fought and killed the lion, but the lion was powerful and mortally wounded Amadi. He died in my arms and asked me to take care of our son and love him as if we both were there doing so. What else can I do? I delivered Abidemi amidst the blood of my husband and the lion. I stayed near the lion's carcass so no other animals would come near." Looking lovingly at her son she continues. "I named him Abidemi Ayotunde Amadi which means 'born during father's absence, joy has returned, and free man. I refused to think negative about my husband's name. He lived free and died free, defending us as a man should do.*

*After I read the letter and cried holding my child close. I went to the Chief. He said that the wrongs of my husband could only be corrected by sacrificing his only son and that I would be able to stay if the child died." I broke in,*

*"I CANNOT BELIEVE THAT!"*

*"But, you cannot possibly believe that, too!"*

*"We have come so far. It is the 1970's not the 1870's. We are in the twentieth-century, all those myths are long gone, aren't they? What about your husband's village? You said you were coming home from there. Could they help?"*

*"I am from this place and you cannot understand the things that go on here, she cried." "You have no idea what is really going on. The chief of my village is the 'Big*

Chief' of all the surrounding villages. What else can I do but what they asked of me? I have no other choice. Where can I go? Of course I don't want to kill my child, I love him. But, what other choice do I have? If I don't do it they will kill him and me. If it has to be done I would rather do it myself than have him endure the life or death that awaits him here."

"Let me help you escape this place, this life, 'his death.'

"I don't know. Where would I go? What would I do?"

She kept glancing at the infant, so I knew her mind was racing trying to find a solution, I wondered how long she had thought about what she was doing just then. It did seem an odd time of day to smother someone. And, why was she here, just off the walking path. Who else did she think would come by this way today? She didn't seem like the impulsive type. But, she didn't 'see' the full picture that I was trying to show her.

"I can take you to America, where you and your children can live in a peaceful state, and you will get to see all the things that are 'wonderful' about life. All the things that were seemingly killed with your husband will be yours for the taking. I am offering you and your child a way to continue living and get out of this miserable existence."

I thought I was doing her a favor. I look back on it now and wonder. I remember the torn expression she had, looking between her now quieted child, me and back toward her village. It was as if she expected the Council of the Chiefs to walk by at any moment. Resignedly, she agreed to go back to the states with me. Throughout the trek through the jungle she kept looking back. It was as if she fully expected someone to stop her from leaving. When we got to the airfield, her eyes grew to the size of small saucers. When the plane took off it was all I could do to stop her from clambering over me and trying to get off the plane. Finally, I got her to settle down, reminding her that if she was upset, the baby would be too. All the way there on the plane I extolled the benefits of Philadelphia, PA USA, better known as the 'City of Brotherly Love'. When we arrived there, it was a rude awakening.

Everyone was not as receptive as I. This woman of color was made to feel like an abhorrence, like no one cared whether she and her child were even there. Some even acted as if they didn't want them, like they were taking something away from them. I had never experienced such rank censure in Philly. The look on her face still *haunts me to this day. It's like that 'deer in the headlights' thing. The deer seems frozen, unaware of the danger, but in reality it is thinking, maybe if I don't move this quizzical light will go away.' One night a long while after that she told me something that broke my heart. "Mind you, I love my son, his siblings, my husband, and my grandchildren. And am grateful that you saved us that long ago day. But, if I had had to make a choice I would have rather been ostracized in my own tongue"*

*When she said it I didn't have a clue what she meant but since that time I have mulled it over quite a bit. She died not long ago and I saw Abidemi again after many years. He was able to shed some light on her words for me.*

*"My mother", he said, "never wanted for me to die, or to leave her home. When she put the bag over my body, she thought the*

rustling sounds were the Council of the Chiefs. They frequently passed by that way at that time of day. She thought if they saw her willingness to follow laws, they would stop her and allow her back into the village. She never wanted me to die. She knew it was their way of testing the strength of a woman. When you came along instead she thought it must be divine intervention, her destiny, and mine.

Upon arriving here she said it frightened her to see the hatred in people's eyes and it made her heart sad that people were treated in such a way, just because of the color of her skin. She so wanted to go home, but didn't know how to voice that to you. She never said these things to me until right before she died. She was afraid I would look at her differently. But, there is not a way I could see her as anything other than what she was, for me. The strong beautiful woman she was.  She sacrificed all she had, all she was for me.

Smilingly, he drifted back into that memory.

I heard her telling my stepfather about what had happened when I was about seven. At the time I didn't understand what she was talking about.  She was pregnant with my sister Special, and she was talking quietly to her husband.  By the age of seven I had learned to be stealthy.  I could move throughout the house without anyone knowing where I was.  I had become adept at not being seen.  My mother used to say that was a gift from my late father.  Don't get me wrong.  My stepfather was kind and loving to me, but my mother made sure I knew about where I came from.  Who my people were, and what type of place I held within that far away system.  She remembered her small village with all their rules and seeming idiosyncrasies, but, their only wish was to survive. They did not have this driving desire to always outdo one another. To have more than your neighbor, instead they tried to help that neighbor when possible. There were no fights over money or land. Just survival, it was as simple as that.

When she came here people only saw another African immigrant, they didn't even try to get to know her before they judged. She missed her home.

After the death of his mother he went home to Africa and has written me several times. He seems happy. He seems to be in the place his mother always wanted him to be. And, the Council of Chiefs considered it a good sign that he is alive and an Agricultural scientist, their crops have never been better. The village is trying to make him one of the Council of Chiefs, the head of it no less.

He said his maternal grandfather wept when he first saw him, the spitting image of his most beloved child. He says his grandfather was beyond himself that day when she disappeared. When the council was delayed with an important matter, they arrived to the site later. He fully expected to find his daughter lying beside a dead infant. He had convinced the council that it was my father's curse and his daughter had proven that the curse would not be continued by having a healthy boy amongst the lion carcass.

He says that he doesn't want to get involved in politics though, he's seen too much of what it can do to a person. I hope that he is where he can find the peace that was almost destroyed by my good intentions. There is an old phrase that goes, 'The road to perdition is paved with good intentions', or something like that. I wonder if my interference brought that wonderful woman unnecessary untold woe. I wonder what would have happened if I hadn't trampled through the jungle that day.

# What do you think?

## It's About Dennis Haysbert A Long Time Ago And Some Books

I know you know Dennis Haysbert. He is that actor that asks you "Are you in good hands?" He has been in several movies, but most women will probably remember him as the cheating husband in, "Waiting to Exhale." He got a bad rep like Danny Glover got from, "The Color Purple." Quite often when women think of Danny Glover, that movie will flash through their mind. And, you know the first thing they want to do is slap the 'Black' off him. Now you know that's a whole lot of smacking. I think the same thing will happen with Dennis Haysbert. I think some obviously pregnant woman is going to walk up to him and say, "You know you ought to be ashamed of yourself, messing 'round' with that heifer with your pregnant wife." Is he even married? That is an interesting line of reasoning though, I am not aware of any other profession where when you get off work, you are not that person anymore. That's just some food for thought for you, something to chew on when your mind is hungry.

Anyway, my story is about another time in history, not the early 21st century, but the early 20th. There was a time when all a man of color was good for was slaving in the field. That time wasn't so long ago we're talking within the last 100 years or so. History may paint a not so clear picture of what really happened. Isn't that always the way? Most of the time there is a clouding of fact by opinion. So I thought I would pitch my cap into the quagmire that is called history. In my version Dennis Haysbert is surrounded by books, but he is outside. The books are time appropriate. They are not the paperback that everyone seems to be buried under today but the tomes of times past, with ridges on the binding, these were real books. I have seen some wallpaper that tries futilely to imitate those old tomes, but doesn't quite give you the full visual. This wasn't that by a long shot. It is a beautiful and awe inspiring sight.

He is standing on the sidewalk, in what looked like old time New York. It was night and he was standing in front of a

Brownstone.  He seemed to be dressed in a suit, a two piece suit, I think.  But, you know then that everyone wore a waistcoat (most of you might know that as a vest), but they were not readily visible if the suit jacket was buttoned.  He wasn't making any effort to stop whatever was going to happen.  Actually come to think about it he seemed very insouciant in his stance.  Leisurely leaning against a banister, or quietly standing in front of one.  Without the look of a frightened child that everyone else seemed to own.  You know that look you get when you hear a crashing sound that is somewhere in your vicinity, and you just know you're going to get blamed for whatever it is that just shattered.  You know you didn't do it but you're only six, and it seems that everything is your fault.

It was as if he was never told that he was supposed to have that look inculcated into his demeanor.  Like there was some class at the little 'colored' schoolhouse that taught it.  And, if you know what is good for you, you better pay rapt attention that day.  Like, even if he didn't get to go to school with the other little 'chillin', his mammy didn't teach him the right lessons at her knee.  Like it wasn't nineteen o' whatever and he didn't have a care in the world.  To quote a period phrase he had a 'nonchalant air' about him. Now you and I both know that that kind of behavior wasn't tolerated from 'the coloreds', 'the darkies', 'the niggers', or whatever else you were called to differentiate you from what was considered 'real' people. I'll never get that. If I call you some derogatory name, does that mean it is apropos, that it defines who you think you are supposed to be?

You could feel the tension. You knew, and held your breath waiting, trying unsuccessfully to be patient. It's like that feeling when you are at the movie and your hand is poised over the popcorn bucket, and your mouth is open, but you just can't seem to get the two to come together. Because, you are scared that in that moment when you inherently close your eyes and begin to chew that you will miss the most vital moment in the whole picture. And, you can't rewind because you're not at your own house. You recognized the scene as that type of moment because there were stacks of books all over the place. You are full of queries. Where did they come from? How did they get here? When were they brought? Who brought them? What are they books about? And of course the most important question. Why are they here?

*I fully intended to approach Mr. Haysbert and ask all those questions at the same time, but something held me back. I think I was standing behind an adjoining brownstone's porch, but I had a very clear view of everything. But, it seemed as if I was invisible. Maybe it was just that from my vantage point I was not visible to anyone. Or maybe it was just that I was invisible because nobody wanted to see me. Not just my physical self, but my soul, my personality, the very essence of who I am. I wonder sometime if other women who were alive then felt that way. Not only us, 'colored' women, but the 'white' women too. Did they sit in the parlors of these affluent homes and disappear? Or were they a formidable force, without reckoning? What about those who are alive now? Are they behind their doors looking out and feeling no one is looking in? In my musing I forgot for a moment that I was about to approach Mr. Haysbert with my questions. I also forgot what that question was. I assumed that it would come back to me once I got my feet to move. I'll let them take care of themselves, they usually do anyway.*

*I returned my attention to the aura that was quickly resurging from the back of my mind where my questions had relegated it. The night was again my focus. The mood was palpable. I could not move, either to run from or toward* whatever was going to arise and overtake the night. It (the night) seemed to know there was something afoot as the old folks say. I wanted to see every change. I watched without the ability to move, the scene was totally enthralling. A good night scene is when you can feel the personality of the night. When it is something that is tangible, thick, heavy, full of promise, of what you cannot surmise. It's as if everything and nothing are going to happen all at the same time, like a silent cacophony. The night had some type of orange glow that permeated the background, kind of like a retouched black and white picture that was taken in the darkest hour. I am on the cusp of a precipice, impatiently waiting with bated breath. What happens next?

## CAN YOU HELP, PLEASE?

# Red

I was dying, or so I thought. All I could see and hear was my son saying, "That's my mother there with the blood on her dress. It seemed that I had blood all down the front of my dress. But only in the middle, as if someone had hollowed me out as you would a melon to make a fruit bowl. But, I didn't feel any pain. If someone had gutted me, wouldn't it hurt some, maybe just a little? Probably not so much, if you're dying I think when you are truly dying your mind is busy trying to find a solution to save you. And, why would there not be any blood spilling over onto my dress or the bed, was I breathing? I don't think so because it looked like a lot of blood and none of it overflowing? Everything besides the dark red blood was white. The dress I wore was white, the sheets, and all around my bed white sheer curtains billowed. It was a stark contrast. I wanted to reach in and touch the place that was bleeding, but I was afraid. I also don't think I could move my arms. They felt as if they weighed 352 lbs. by themselves. My son wore the traditional male garb, the diaper like loin cover, and, nothing else.

Just a side note I have a gorgeous son if I must say so myself. He has turned out to be a wonderful man. I hope I get to tell him that I am so very proud of him and how much I love him.

We were royalty but I could not tell you how we got to be. I don't remember anything but that moment and my son standing over my prone form yelling at a person who could only have been a slave. The fact that my very affectionate son seemed afraid to touch me solidified my impression of the situation, I was dying. Why aren't you helping her? That was his impassioned plea. The slave reverently said, "I have no intention of touching the royal one, I am not trained and I don't know what happened to her." I grew weaker and barely heard that last statement. "If you don't do something and she dies it will be your life forfeited next. You will be fodder under her body if I bury her today". "I wonder whatever happened to that man. If it were me I would have eased out of the castle while the prince was taking care of his mother. But, you know most people wouldn't have done that, they would have just stayed there and prayed that the queen would be okay. Oddly thinking, if she does end up being ok, and I am gone they will blame whatever happened on me. And, if she does die, do I deserve to live? I wonder where that lies between misplaced loyalty and self preservation."

Now that I am almost fully recovered it is my goal to find out what exactly happened to me that I ended up in this predicament. I will start with the earlier part of the day. I was preparing for a celebration of some sort. It was not an anniversary or anything like that. I think I remember it being special for some unique reason that would not recur. Someone within the royal house had done something worthy of celebrating. I remember that because of the white dress that I was wearing. It was of the traditional garb of the royal family worn on just such occasions. On other regular days we might have worn outfits with white components, but not all white, and only white. Why do we associate white with most good and black with most bad? Is it tradition or training? Maybe it is the reference throughout time to good things being associated with being white. I'll have to research that more, later, once I get my footing back.

All the royal extended family had been invited as well. Which one of these relatives was the one who had tried to end my life? I wonder where my husband is. I wonder if he is living or dead. He is probably living because there would have been some evidence of him being hurt by now, wouldn't there? There are quite a few things that I cannot recall. Everyone says that I lost so much blood that if affected my memory. There is a friend that I have that I will ask what she recalls about that day, if anything. I hope that she can tell me what really happened.

"What did anyone have against me that they would try on this auspicious day to do me in?" There are so many questions that are as yet unanswered.

Sometime later I find out that my friend apparently knows no more than I do. This is curious. She is always with me. I wonder where she was that day. What really happened? Will I ever know what is going on? OH! I know who did this to me, but I will never get the opportunity to tell anyone because I really am dying. Now I realize that instead of my whole lived life flashing before my eyes, my whole rest of my life that I will not ever get to enjoy is what I am seeing. I never understood what the statement, "Never do we imagine that the day of our death is a day that has already begun," meant until today. It means that you must not waste your time wondering what to do about yesterday or tomorrow, JUST LIVE TODAY. Stop wishing and dreaming about what you think your life should be, JUST LIVE TODAY. Stop wondering how your neighbor got whatever it is that they have, JUST LIVE TODAY. Remember my tale of woe, JUST LIVE TODAY. Well, I'd like to spend more time with you, but I am really dying. I hope my son will find out who killed me and ensure that they are brought to justice. It has been wonderful spending time with you, and if you don't take anything away from our time together remember this, JUST LIVE TODAY.

# Just Live Today

# PSYCHOSIS

*"Wow, this place was ginormous, isn't that the word the kids use now-a-days." It was bigger than gigantic, larger than enormous, greater than humungous. I had never seen a place bigger than this. I didn't think there were places built this big, that were houses. Which begs the question, are we in a house or some rented out ballroom? I will have to ask around and see if I can get an idea, all my neighbors and acquaintances were there. And, every person I knew from work was there. Also, there were some young people from other aspects of my life too. It was so overwhelming that I don't even remember driving here, or getting out of the car. Once I stepped inside it was like a whole new world. I looked around and couldn't see the end of the party; you know how sometime you can look to the end of the room and see the walls. Well, I couldn't even distinguish where the walls were. Maybe if I mingle some I can get a glimpse of where the wall is the people are packed in here so tight. You know what this feels like, being lost at sea. You find yourself thinking, is there an end to the water. I was asking myself. Is there an end to the bodies? Obviously, there is not.*

*The music, however, even though I couldn't see the band, permeated the entire place and seemed to shake the foundations. Again, I don't know how I got to the supermarket portion of the building and who that man I was with was. He seemed to know me and we seemed to be dating, but also, seemed not to have ever met me before that very moment. Is that 'déjà vu' or some other foreign colloquialism? Have you ever met someone on the street and had that thought. Saying to yourself, "I know I know this person, but from where?" Usually several days later when you are just about to drift off to sleep, and the person is nowhere to be found, you go, Oh! That is who that was. But, you never tell the person because whenever you're around you never think of that bedtime thought.*

*One of my old supervisors came over and I stopped him because he had a sandwich roll in his hand, and I wanted a piece of it before he went back into the melee. He said I should get a piece quickly, but I couldn't seem to find anything to put it on. All of a sudden, he got very tired, emotionally. He wasn't tired in any physical way but it seemed his spirit was tired and he didn't have any more fight in him. He rested his head in the crook in my neck. But, amazingly, there was no sexual connotation felt. It was similar to a young child resting there when the world has made him weary. I know anyone who has kids or has spent any significant amount of time around any knows exactly what I am talking about. A small child will go and go and go, then all of a sudden will lay their head on whatever solid object is near and go to sleep.*

*As I walked down each aisle he seemed to walk alongside me just enjoying the peacefulness of being there. The man that I* now surmised was my beau, was at times in the buggy with the groceries and others walking beside it.

Once my old supervisor was gone, I remember seeing a couple of young ladies I knew. It seemed they were trying to find the restroom. I was able to tell them where it was. I remembered going there and looking around. Even the restroom was inordinately large. There were several rows of stalls and then some kind of curtain separating another section of stalls that were different. There were fewer of them and they were larger than the others.

Just beyond that was an odd place where there were foreign women scantily clad practicing some unknown black magic looking dance. That was the only thing that popped into my head. I am sure that there wasn't anything like that going on, but all I ever had as a reference was old movies where the only time you saw these types of dances was when some kind of voodoo was going on. I didn't look further, I think because I think I was afraid of what I would see.

They went into the restroom and I don't remember seeing them anymore, but I didn't think anything about it because the place was so big. I was still in the supermarket and telling my beau that he shouldn't persist in playing the games he did. He would pretend to be shy and hide his face while lying on his side. All of a sudden we were in a room behind the restroom and there was something very strange going on. There was a man there with that same type of voodooesc look. His face was painted and he was barely wearing anything. The man was going around the room putting thin ropes around the necks of the persons lying around on the floor. When we had come into the room we saw a young woman that was being dragged away into an alcove. She looked like she had been bludgeoned. You couldn't see any actual bruises but you could see that here spirit was bedraggled. Remember I told my beau to stop playing the game where he acted shy, well, it seemed that that was the sign to the voodoo guy that you were accepting of having the thin rope put around your neck. Apparently there was some kind of extremely strong topical anesthetic on the rope and as soon as it interacted with the skin it completely knocked the person unconscious.

Upon waking I felt like my mind and head were forming anew and I could see them doing so. It was reminiscent of one of those digitally enhanced movies that show the reconstruction of a skull block by block on a computer screen. But as my skull formed something very strange happened.

Instead of being me I was masculine in formation and I had glasses. Didn't my beau look like this? All of sudden I realized that all of this had been a dream and I was really the man with not only the thin rope around my neck, but some kind of constriction device around my face. It reminded me of the cone that they put around a dog's head to keep him from biting.

As the enormity of the situation struck me, I woke up and realized that all of it was a dream.

# Have you ever had a dream like that?

# There Was A Whole 'Nother House

I want to tell you about a strange and wondrous house
I think it was constructed in the antebellum south
There are columns inside as tall as a tree
Oh, you can't see it, let me show you, come along with me
Look here and there, the white of the walls is pristine
It is a domicile befitting a king or a queen
But, not everyone gets to see the inside, here
Because it's filled with wickedness, cruelty, and fear
You see, the old slave master occupied this space
I recall his overgrown belly, the bulbous jowls of his face
I saw it in a picture, somewhere on the second floor
You'll be able to see it too, that and much more
I was told he spit when he spoke and coughed when he'd
laugh
He liked the young colored girls he owned, called them 'staff'
His belly was as large as the one on his potbellied stove
He was high and mighty because of the horses he drove
Depending on where you're from they might be called cattle
The slaves he owned might be referred to as chattel
This house was constructed with perniciousness in mind

He wanted to live in the dwellings reminiscent of his kind
On the outside the house was all white and clean
But there is a door in the library that remains unseen
It leads off into a labyrinthine of passageways
Where you might be taken and until death there might stay
Very few have returned hearty and whole from within
You see, they were not the same as when they went in
From what they endured, something in their soul is mired
They were defeated, haggard, bedraggled. Worn, and tired
There's a whole 'nother house is what they're prone to say
Nothing else, because what happens there, there must stay
Gone are the embellishments that you see around
All that's there is darkness and the blight of cold ground
This beauteous scene before your eyes today
Has a foundation hewn out from deep rich red clay
The rich oak and pine that adorn this interior
Is just window dressing to hide motives ulterior
The chairs, armoires, rugs, tables, and things
Don't completely cover horrors that going beneath bring
There is a whole 'nother house, you don't believe me do you
Well I have it on good authority, and know it's true
One day when my greatest grandmother was a child
With pickaniny braids, and a youthful spirit mild
She snuck into the back door down by the kitchen
Past the ladies auxiliary club in the parlor stitchen'
She was quiet as a mouse because if she got caught

A whippin' was what even the slightest nosiness brought
So silently she crept in the wake of her mother
Because she was enamored of her like no other
So she followed her into the big house on the hill
And froze when the men looked around quite still
She hid behind the big statue of a general, maybe General
Lee
She had no idea who it was, it was ok, it didn't matter you
see
Look over there, right there I think that may be the one
It does look like Lee, or maybe it's the old master's son
But there she stood and didn't move, frozen with fright
Because she couldn't believe the things within her sight
Her mother was silent and still which was puzzling
She was always smiling, talking, her baby's neck nuzzling
There were so many books, more than she had ever seen
She was in awe for a moment, her mother silently screamed
She had noticed her daughter, but couldn't warn her
To go back, get out, run away, look no further
With her eyes she motioned toward the door
But her daughter's attention was hers no more
She was focused intently, on the book that was moved
So she could follow them, innocence curiosity had been
infused
You could still see the sparkle, gleaming in her young eyes
The house and the furnishings, all of it had her hypnotized

The sprawling staircase that she had come past
Seemed to reach up to heaven, and last and last
The shiny floor that almost made her slip
Making her step lively, concentrate biting her lip
She had no idea because she had never been inside
But wanted to know why her mother sometimes cried
Mom left her with Mamabell and went up to the house
Mamabell said, "Mind yours" with a snort and a grouse
She'd say there are some things you don't want to know
Some places you really, really don't want to go
I'd complain, it's so pretty, with all those windows to see
She'd say every shiny thing is not good for me
That day when the men came to take mama to the house
My chance came, sweet opportunity, I acted the louse
Mamabell fell asleep of course, and I had to sneak out
I had to see what was inside what's all the fuss about
I knew exactly where they were going you see
So I snuck around the back way, going through the trees
From the back of the house I didn't see her come in
But there were so many places to hide in the huge kitchen
I heard them in the hallway, not mom, only the men
Talking to the master, arrogantly, spitefully telling him
"Yeah this is the one you requested right here
She resisted 'cause her pickaniny was near"
"Gal, you know you better come when I call, right
I don't care if it's the middle of the night"

My mother didn't answer and I wondered why
She just averted her eyes, let tears fall and heaved a sigh
They then dragged her into the library, I though what
Are they going to make her look something up
I had forgotten a whisper that I heard long ago
There is a whole 'nother house and you don't want to go
She told my father, and he was enraged
Paced the room, like back and forth, like a lion caged
She calmed him reminding him there was no other way
Think of the 'chillin honey, where'd we go we have to stay
He bellowed, he was crying, saying he didn't even care
She quietly asked him what she would do if he wasn't there
'Cause you know what they would do
They wouldn't hesitate to make me watch as they killed you
He said they were taking away his ability to be a man
He was a warrior, a proud and mighty African
Standing behind the statue all this ran through her mind
There is a whole 'nother house, returned in kind
She tentatively moved the book as she'd seen the man do
The door slid open silently and she slid through
It closed behind her and darkness took over
She clung to the wall so she wouldn't fall over
Her eyes adjusted and further on down the path
She heard her mother's whimper and the master's laugh
She was very quiet because she knew somehow
If they found her it would not be good for anyone now

She wondered if Mamabell had awoken, scared
Because she was gone, and her father wasn't there
He was out in the fields with the other men
Not the Whites but all the Africans
There were a few Whites there to keep the peace
They were mean and yelled and beat without cease
Very soon she would have to go to the fields to pick
Almost big enough to pluck cotton from the stick
But this day was like all that had come before
Except she was underground scared, where was that door
She moved forward because she couldn't go back
She couldn't see, the firelight was becoming slack
She crept along the wall and almost screamed
The wall gave way to a gruesome scene
Her mother was below her spread out on a table
Eyes warily scanning the room as much as she was able
She caught sight of me, a sob was wrenched from her soul
Closing her eyes against the master's cajole
He was speaking soft words as the men stood around
She kept her eyes closed and didn't make a sound
Master was out of sight so I looked around this place
There were other paths and rooms that filled this space
I could hear that there was other things goings on
But I was scared to move praying singing a silent song
I heard things that no young girl should ever hear
There was a whole 'nother house, and I was here

Master was making a strange grunting sound
I couldn't see him as the other men stood around
It seemed an eternity that I stood frozen
Because I had followed, a disobedient path I had chosen
When they finished whatever they were doing to her
They roughly grabbed my crying, broken mother
They didn't even notice me plastered against the wall
She knew though that I had seen and heard it all
I followed closer than I had before
Because I didn't want to get caught in that door
When it closed I slid behind the statue once more
They were no longer in a hurry, having done their gore
My mother's shoulders shook with silent tears
I had no idea that I was the center of her fears
They left the room and rousted her back to her quarters
I left, going through now lackluster borders
I ran through the trees screaming a silent cacophony
Why didn't I listen when they tried to tell me
That I didn't want to know what lay within
But I thought I knew better raising my chin
My mother was there when I arrived
Mamabell had since gone, mad I surmised
My mother just looked at me, she didn't utter a word
She just grabbed me an hugged me tightly, how absurd
From that day till the day she died
I watched her, seeing the tracks of the tears cried

There is a whole 'nother house under this shiny veneer
The book that opens the door is right here
It is ironic too, the name of the book
"House beautiful" there it is take a look
I only know that story you see
Because this house you're in now belongs to me
I have walked the labyrinth below many times
Hearing the screams, whimpers like gilded wind chimes
I don't show everyone who takes this tour all of it
But since I have shared my story, I will not here quit
I can imagine that you have heard other tales
About a whole 'nother house, others regale
But I know the truth from the ones who lived here
There're other southern homes like this one, far and near
I'll show you if you want to see with your own eyes
If in your imagination you can other's plight surmise
And then upon hearing there is a whole 'nother house said
You'll be a believer, perk your ears up raise your head
You can ask your brethren that are older but wise
About the stories told by the elders about past lives

# Ask them about a whole 'nother house

# HE KILLED ME

"I can't believe he has that incredulous look on his face." He is just standing there asking that ridiculous question. "Even though she got shot because you were trying to kill me?" Is he really talking to that trifling hoe, after she just shot me? Forreal! I don't think so, I think the question is rhetorical. It is the age old story. Boy meets girl, boy likes girl, girl likes boy. Then reality sets in. I am laying there in the middle of the mall and he is standing over me looking foolish. The woman is so familiar, and yet she is a stranger to me. I have never met her, but as the old saying goes, "There, but for the grace of God, go I." As I lay there feeling the blood slowly seep out of me I thought, "This is so much like a reality show." It should be called, "The real people of real life." Because, as you and I both know the word 'real' in the title of any show makes you wonder, are these people really real on any level. Are they, 'real' actors even? I almost laughed, but remembered at the last possible moment that it would hurt beyond what was already unbearable. Whenever you're hurt you wonder how long a minute is. You think, 'I am going to die here and it will happen just before the people get here to help me. I think we are taught that from school. Prime example: Shakespeare, "Romeo and Juliet", need I say more. How many times has that been remade into a movie of the week? I met this 'boy' about five years ago. I know, I know, I look fifteen. But, in 'reality' I am almost thirty. You would think that at this age I would know better, as they say. I would know 'when to say when. But, all I wanted was a "Refill" as Elle would say. If you don't know that song just imagine what it is about, and you got it. He is my drink and I decided to 'pour my own poison'. Well, anyway, I knew his reputation when I met him. Maybe not, you know sometime when you meet someone new you don't even give ear to rumors and supposition. Which begs the question, how much of what you hear about someone should you believe. Someone probably 'neglected' to make me hear what they were trying to get me to hear. They say love is blind, is it deaf too? "Helen Keller" aka love please stand up. So, he is five years older than me and acts ten years younger. Are all men cursed to mature slower than women, or is it that we as women allow them to think that idiotic behavior is cool and cute? I think it is a mixture of the two, because I have seen some mature ten year old boys and some infantile thirty fives. Maybe it's just that the ten year olds haven't hit puberty yet. I think I should do a survey. I must not be dying for real because I've heard that when you are your whole life flashes before your eyes, nope, just the last year or so. About a year ago, the blinders started to slip and the wax started draining. As I lay here I try to keep my eyes closed and not think about this situation. I can hear someone telling me to keep my eyes open and talk to them. I think they think because I have my eyes closed that I am giving up. No such thing is going on here. I am trying to focus on the scenery that is replaying behind my eyes. Also, I am trying not to open them and see the scenery that is in front of my eyes. There is a woman that is lying next to me and I don't know if she is living or dead. And all the man I thought loved me can do is stand over me trying to figure out what to say next. I don't want you to say anything. I want you to do something. Stop being dumbfounded and call the police. Too late, some woman already took care of it. She saw that you were in a stupor and took over. Isn't that always the way? As women, most of us anyway, when it is not being taken care of by the man, we do it. That makes it hard sometime for the good men. Because usually by the time we get to the good one, we are so used to taking care of it, we have a hard time relinquishing our supposed reign. That is not what happened here. Don't get me wrong I think he is a good man, but he never tried to take over the 'manly' things. That should have been my first clue that something was awry. In every person's life I think, there are things that are red flags. I think we just have to stop being color blind and be honest with ourselves about our idiosyncrasies. Own yours. It has taken this travesty to make me look closely and begin to own mine. No there was not a misspelling or misuse of the word 'tragedy'. The difference here is that this was not something that accidently happened, i.e. a tragedy.

It just accidently happened to the wrong person.  One of my idiosyncrasies is that I walk around in rose colored glasses and forget that the world is full of grays and oranges.  This guy, was not 'that guy', you know the one that everyone looks at and can't quite figure out.  The one that is just good, he doesn't cheat, beat, or usually even have cross words with his wife, he is an anomaly, the antithesis of what a 'player' is.  This is that other guy, the one who thought he was because a few girls told him that he was the man.  He thought this because, his 'boys' patted him on the back, instead of telling him the truth about what he was supposed to be doin' with a 'woman' like me.  At least that is the thought that ran through my mind, and was running through it now.  I wonder also, if it went even deeper.  Aren't our sons what our mothers teach them to be?  Are they the products of experience or knowledge?  Do they take more from daddies or mommas?  Those questions seem moot in the light that I had met his mother and father and neither of them seem to be the cause of 'what', rather who is standing before me today.  I push my mind away from all these thoughts that I should have had yesterday and ask myself, the right question, what now?"

# What now

# It's New Fangled Police Tactics In The Old Fangled South

"I can't believe this is happening to me. This is the 1970's not the 1880's. I thought we as a people (that phrase is about being human and not about what color my skin is) had moved beyond this type of nonsense. I am just flabbergasted at what this 'pig' has been doin' to me." He is on me like white on rice. I live in Boston, that's South Boston, Virginia. I know, I know you thought I was talkin' 'bout the one in the north, but you wrong."

"Don't let my fancy talk confuse you, this is the 'south'. You ever heard the expression, 'true north'. Well, this here, what I'm tellin' is of the 'true south'. We got some 'pigs' aka 'the fuzz' aka 'polices' round here that think that they still in the antebellum south, but try to put on the 'airs' that they are ahead o' they times. They just as back in the day as all us other 'regular' folks, I usually don't call folks normal 'cause, hey, if every person is supposed to be an individual, who in the world is 'normal'. Okay, okay where was I? I was either at the beginning or the end, but I will start over. My story begins with the break – in. I was out one enenin' and when I got home my do' was open. Now I know some folks would waltz right in and investigate on they own, but not this gal, she doesn't do that. I know when I'm outa' my element. I walked right down to da' police station and grabbed the biggest one I could see.

As we was walking back, he was checkin' me out cus', you know I look good and everythang'. He said, "I'm surprised a fine quality chick' like you live in dis' here' neighborhood. I thought only sisters' and brothers' lived here." I didn't say anything because I didn't feel the need to. I jes' smiled and let him go on thinking whatever he wanted. My mama used to say, "You cain't control what another person thinks about you, it's about what you think about yo'self that matters. I do sometime wonder why people don't jes aks me, if they want to know.

He hed' made the same mistake most people make when they meet me. Assuming that I was white and not colored' or black' dependin' on what part of the neighborhood' you from. I know there is a lot of others like me. They call us passers. That mean if we want to us can go for white. I usually don't care either way, but I knew dat' if this 'pig knew now that I wasn't white the way he lookin' at me, that might jes' change the whole sitiation'. I was thinkin' maybe if I jus' don't say nothing I can get this 'pig to look around and see what is going on at my pad' and then he can be on his merry way.

I don't need any more 'anything' in my life. 'Specially not the 'man'. Everybody know that once you got not only a man, but 'the man' in yo' business. You cain't have no business. It's not that I want to do anything that is against the law, but I do like to live my life like I want.

So this 'pig', I ain't gon' tell y'all his name, cus' I know somma' y'all know him, checked out my crib and gave it the thumbs up. Whoever had been there was gone. Nothin' was missing 'cept my pride. I felt foolish at havin' gon and got him. But, then again, I'd rather be foolish than dead. I offer him a drink, just some water or juice, maybe even milk, not no strong stuff, cus' she doesn't do that. A lot of my friends drink, but, I figure if I'm gon act silly, I can do so without corroding my liver. Just a thought fo' some of y'all to ponder. He said, "Maybe not, I should get back to the station. You do live awful close to the station. Maybe sometime I could come round and check up on you?"

I stood there I know for a full minute with my mind racing to find a good answer (that's one that says "NOT" without gettin' me hauled back around the corner to the jail), "Well, uh, I'm in a situation," I stammered. "I don't think so," the 'pig' shot right back. Cus' I know if you had some beau, you wouldda' called him, cus who wants to walk through the streets at this time with a cop on they arm? Nobody, das' who, so what is it, you don't like me?" I replied a little too quickly, "It's not that, I couldn't call him, cus' the phone is in here, an' I shole' wasn't comin' in here to call." I added a little neck rollin' to prove my point.

He chuckled, "I know it's hard to imagine walkin round here with a flatfoot on your arm, look I'll make it easy for you, I'll pick you up at eight on Friday. Don't be late or I'll have to arrest you," he said laughingly. I didn't know him well enough to tell if he was jokin' or serious, so you know I was ready. "You look good enough to eat," he said wolfishly taking in my outfit. "You hungry," I nervously replied. "Naw' it ain't that, I just think you look beautiful, I just ain't too good with words, that's all. During dinner he explained to me his life and his philosophy. He said that, and I quote,

"Every person is right in their feelings." I didn't understand at all what that meant, and I guess my face told on me because he held up his hand and said, "Wait for it, but wrong in their actions." He went on to explain that it wasn't the feelings of a person that made them do bad things, it was the actions. I thought about that for a moment and then said, "I disagree, because it is the feelings that drive the actions." "Okay, but whatever happened to self control, and compassion?" He replied. "What," I asked, because there was a look of complete and utter shock on his face now. "No one has ever contradicted me before, I am not sure I like it." "Well, like it or not, I am not going to just agree to anything you say just because you're a cop, or just because you said it. She is not that girl," I said pointing to myself. Later, as he dropped me off he said, "I am so glad I kinda' bullied you into going out with me." "Kinda, how you gon' say that. You gave me no choice." But, I was laughing when I said it. "You might have guessed that it is not so easy to 'bully' me into anything.

# Ima' let y'all work on what happens then

CICELY TYSON WAS THERE
AND            THAT                    OTHER
ACTRESS,
YOU KNOW THE ONE
WHO PLAYS THE MOTHER IN
"WHAT'S LOVE GOT TO DO WITH IT?"

I THINK I HAVE THAT SAME VISION EVERY ONCE IN A WHILE
YOU KNOW THE ONE, IT MAKES YOU THINK, MAKES YOU SMILE
I WONDER WHATEVER HAPPENED TO HONEY CHILD
IS SHE NEAR, UP THE ROAD, OR DOWN THE WAY A MILE
WAY BACK WHEN, A LONG TIME AGO, COME TO THINK
WHEN WOMEN WORE DRESSES AND MEN BOUGHT THE DRINK
WHEN EVERYTHING WASN'T FOR SALE, LOVE DIDN'T STINK
MY MAN CAME HOME WITH A COAT, A HUNDRED PERCENT MINK
HE WOULDN'T TELL ME HOW THAT GIFT CAME TO BE
AND JUST WHY HE WAS IMPARTING IT TO ME
I THOUGHT, I WANT TO KEEP IT AND GUARDED IT JEALOUSLY
IT MADE ME FEEL BETTER, I FIT INTO SOME OTHER CATEGORY
I WANTED TO QUERY, ASK, YOU GOT IT WHERE
WOULD THE ANSWER INCLUDE, CICELY TYSON WAS THERE
AND OTHERS ABOUT WHOM YOU MIGHT NOT CARE
AND, SOME WHO MIGHT MAKE YOU STOP AND STARE
YOU KNOW THAT ACTRESS WHO PLAYED THE MOTHER
IN SEVERAL MOVIES I'VE COME TO DISCOVER
SHE WAS THERE, HER NAME SOMETHING OR ANOTHER
IN "WHAT'S LOVE GOT TO DO WITH IT" SHE SLIGHTLY DID SMOTHER
BUT I THINK SHE IS A GREAT ACTRESS, TOO
SHE COULD HANG OUT WITH MAYA, CICELY, AND THAT CREW
SHE BRINGS TO EACH CHARACTER SOMETHING NEW
AND DOES PROFESSIONALISM CONTINUOUSLY IMBUE
BUT LET'S GET BACK TO MY TALE, IT IS A SIDE SPLITTER
WITH THIS COAT ON HIS ARM, HE CAME ALL IN A TITTER
LIKE HE WAS FIFTEEN, JUST KISSED THE BABY SITTER

NOT DEEP IN THOUGHT, BUT WITH THOUGHTS ALL ATWITTER
I THOUGHT IF I ASKED, HE'D WRINKLE HIS FOREHEAD
AND LOOK AT ME SIDEWAYS, WITH IMMINENT DREAD
I DON'T WANT TO SEE THAT LOOK, NO, I'D RATHER BE DEAD
SO I WAS QUIET, AND ADMIRED MY COAT INSTEAD
I HAD NEVER EVEN SEEN ANYTHING LIKE THIS
SO I TURNED IT THIS WAY AND FELT BLISS
IT WAS AKIN TO THE FIRST TIME YOU GET A REAL KISS
LET ME TELL YOU THE REST OF THE STORY, I AM BEING REMISS
I THINK CICELY TYSON REPRESENTED SOMEONE
WHO WAS SERIOUS, NOT MESSING AROUND UNTIL THE WORK IS DONE
NOT THAT SHE DOESN'T KNOW HOW TO HAVE FUN
BUT, IF YOU'RE ABOUT NONSENSE, SHE IS NOT THE ONE
THE OTHER ACTRESS, JENNIFER LEWIS IS HER NAME
SHE HOLDS HER OWN IN THE ACTING GAME
SHE WASN'T UNSCRUPULOUS, SHE EARNED HER FAME
I KNOW SHE'S PROUD, ANYTHING LESS WOULDN'T HAVE BEEN THE SAME
BOTH OF THEM WERE THERE THE DAY I GOT MY COAT
BUT I WASN'T OBNOXIOUS, I DIDN'T GLOAT
I COULDN'T CONTAIN MY WONDER, MY REACTION WASN'T ROTE
BUT IT WASN'T OVER THE TOP, I HELD TO THE RIGHT NOTE
MY COAT WAS AN UNEXPECTED BUT TREASURED POSSESSION
I WORE IT EVERY CHANCE I GOT, LEADING AN IMAGINARY PROCESSION
I ENVISIONED GREAT THINGS, THOUGHT OF A DIFFERENT PROFESSION
AT TIMES I EVEN FELT GUILTY, BUT DIDN'T DIVULGE THAT IN CONFESSION
I FORGOT ALL THE THINGS THAT HAD FORGONE THAT GIFT, COME
BEFORE
RECEIVING LESS AND LESS, GIVING MORE AND MORE
NEVER WANDERING INTO TOMORROW, SURMISING WHAT'S IN STORE
HIDING THE SCARS, THE STRAIN, THE FRACTURE, THE GORE
SOMETIME I THINK BACK ON THAT FATEFUL DAY
TRYING TO REMEMBER WHY I DIDN'T KNOW JUST WHAT TO SAY
THINKING CAN I BE BOUGHT IN SUCH A WAY
OR AM I WORTH MORE THAN THIS, WILL THIS MAKE ME STAY
CICELY LOOKED AT ME AND REPEATED SOME OF HER FAMOUS WORDS
SOMETHING TO THE AFFECT OF, THIS IS VERY ABSURD
YOU ARE WORTH SO MUCH MORE, HADN'T YOU HEARD
DON'T LET SOME MAN COME AND TREAT YOU LIKE A TURD
JENNIFER, JUMPED ON THE BANDWAGON THEN
SHE SAID WHEN YOU GON' REALIZE YOU'RE A DIAMOND GIRL, WHEN
I STOOD THERE HOLDING MY COAT CLOSE LETTING THEIR WORDS SINK
IN
AND JUST AS THEY WERE GOING TO SAY SOMETHING AGAIN

I SAID WAIT DON'T I HAVE THE RIGHT TO DECIDE
IF I WILL STAND AND FIGHT, OR RUN AND HIDE
BECAUSE THAT WAS WHAT I WAS TOLD, HAD EVERYBODY LIED
OR DID MY NIGHTMARES AND YOUR DREAMS JUST COLLIDE
THE THING I AM TRYING TO TELL SOME YOUNG GIRL
IS, DON'T LET SOME MATERIAL THING COME IN AND PUT YOU IN A WHIRL
TURN YOU AROUND LIKE A MERRY-GO-ROUND, SET YOU IN A TWIRL
MAKE YOU SICK YOUR STOMACH, MAKE YOU WANT TO HURL
ALL THAT GLITTERS DEFINITELY IS NOT GOLD
REMEMBER BE YOURSELF, ALLOW THE TRUTH TO BE TOLD
MAKE HIM BE DECENT, TO HAVE AND TO HOLD
MAKE HIM TREASURE YOU UNTIL YOU'RE OLD
DON'T LET HIM BUY HIS WAY OUT OF APOLOGIZING RIGHT
HOLD OUT FOR IT, DON'T GIVE IT UP ON THE FIRST NIGHT
LET HIM ILLUMINATE YOUR LIFE, ALSO BE HIS LIGHT
HEAR WITH YOUR HEART, NOT WHAT'S IN PLAIN SIGHT
DON'T LET HIM BY YOU LIKE YOU'RE CHEAP
OR CONVINCE YOU THAT YOUR DEMANDS ARE TOO STEEP
HOLD ON TO YOUR SELF RESPECT, AND THE RIGHT MAN KEEP
NOT THE WOLF THAT LOOKS LIKE A SHEEP
BE IN LOVE WITH HIM NOT WHAT HE CAN BUY
MAKE HIM LOVE YOU AS WELL IF YOU WANT HIM TO BE YOUR GUY
THERE WILL BE TIMES THAT HE WILL IRRITATE, MAKE YOU ASK WHY
LET ME SAY, THE ANSWER IS, HE MAKES YOUR HEART FLY
LET MY STORY BE A CAUTIONARY TALE
LET LOVE BE YOUR GUIDE AND YOU CANNOT FAIL
AGAINST THE MATERIAL, FIGHT TO THE END, REGALE
DO NOT CARRY AROUND THE SIGN, FOR SALE
I THINK ABOUT MY COAT EVERY ONCE IN A WHILE
IT WAS VERY NICE, QUITE CHIC I MEAN IT WAS IN STYLE
BUT I DIDN'T THINK ABOUT IT ON THE DAY I WENT TO CHARGES FILE
I RAN FROM MY HOME, I FELT LIKE I HAD RUN A MILE
HE DIDN'T LOVE ME THE WAY I DESERVED, NO HE HIT
IN MY VISION CICELY TYSON SAYS, HUSH CHILD, COME, SIT
THAT OTHER ACTRESS SAID WHY YOU HAVING SUCH A FIT
YOU KNOW THE ONE, THE MOM FROM "WHAT'S LOVE GOT TO DO WITH
IT"

# WHAT DO YOU COST

# Didn't I Try To Tell You

I know that any woman out there with a daughter can relate to the following question, that I repeatedly seem to ask my daughter. **Didn't I try to tell you.....etc?**
According to your circumstances, you know what comes next. What the total question is. Allow me to tell you a sad tale about that question and how it sometimes goes unanswered. I wonder, does it ignominiously fall by the wayside, at the resurgence of more pertinent queries. Does it become redundant if it is in the aftermath of some catastrophe that occurs? Or does it regale against circumstance. I'll let you ruminate on that cob for a bit while I reminisce for a moment. I remember it as if it was last night. It is interesting to me the way memories replay. Sometime they are as clear as a bell, sometime they are as clear as mud. What is the determining factor in each case? I think that the individuals mind decides which we want

to remember and how.  So many questions, so little time to have them answered completely.

We had recently moved, I remember because there seemed to be an overflow of boxes.  It seemed that there was a well worn path through the boxes to the door and throughout the house what seemed to be a box obstacle course. When you first view a new home it seems huge, but once you put all the things that make up your memories into it, it seems so much more infinitesimal.  It was late, the man (also known as my husband) had already went to 'bed'.  That meant that he had retired to the bedroom and the TV, feeling that he had contributed enough in reference to the move.  He had done all the 'real' work.  His 'part' was the moving of the sofa and all the other 'heavy' stuff, aka the furniture.  The door to my bedroom was off to the left side of the living room, was that the desired end of the box maze?  When the boxes had been brought in had he orchestrated the placing of the boxes so they left an avenue to the bedroom, hmm?

Anyway, my daughter seemed to be the only one who was impervious to the over abundance of boxes. Being almost six feet tall she towered over the box tower.  She was heading toward the door to open it.  I can't recall if there was a knock at the door or we had a doorbell.  I said to her, "don't open the door, let your dad come and get it".  She just kept on walking, like I hadn't spoken at all.  It seemed as though she didn't even hear me and she proceeded to the door.  Like she knew who it was and why they were there.  Did she?  So, she opened it and immediately started yelling something, now it seemed to be my turn to not be able to hear.  Although I was very close to her, I was standing in the middle of the 13 x 10 living room.  I could see her struggling to keep whoever it was out of the house.

Time seemed to slow down.  She seemed to be putting up a valiant effort to deny our late night guest.  I was torn as to what to do.  My mind said, "Multitask".  I started yelling to my husband and moving toward the door to lend my shoulder to that endeavor.  I had just taken my first step as the man broke through my daughter's defenses my husband comes running from our bedroom shouting, "What is all the ruckus, in here?  And, why is my daughter trying to keep you out."  It seemed as though everything was still moving in slow motion.  I couldn't believe that he had broken through the door.  It seemed flimsy, even though it was an exterior door.  It seemed to bend under his pressure.  I think that was just my over imaginative mind playing tricks on me.  Once he got into the room pandemonium ensued.  I saw the knife come from his jacket pocket, it was just a silvery glint of metal, I wasn't even sure it was real. Then he had pushed my daughter aside and was coming straight toward me.

Now that I think about it I think that he knew that it would hurt her more if I were hurt than if she was. I saw the knife go down at the left side of my chest near my shoulder, but I didn't feel any pain. Adrenalin kicked in and I wrenched the weapon from him and began jabbing it into his throat and slicing his neck. It all happened so fast, but seemed interminable. It was as if I was outside myself watching. Therein lies the danger of reflex actions. If I had just taken the knife and thrown it away, my soul would not still cry today. He seemed insurmountable. Before long though he slumped against my husband's shoulder, all the fight in him, spent.

I figured out who it was and thought, I know this 'boy', when did he become so capricious. What happened to make him so avaricious, so angry? Why? Why? There were tears in my eyes and all I remember saying was, "Why are you doing this, what is going on. I didn't realize that I had been stabbed. It still didn't hurt. Why had my body not recognized that it had been pierced? That it had been irrevocably changed in that instant, and not for the better. But, I think adrenalin kicked in and took over because all that I could think about was this 'boy' that I had done in.  And, there was no doubt in my mind that he was through.  I wondered why he had done what he had, and queried, was there any other way I could have gone.  Well the first question will never have an answer. But as to the second question

I'll leave that to you, to ponder

# A Parting Thought

I chose this font so that I could end this
missive the way I artistically began,

I hope you can read it, and my words
completely understand

All the things that are written already
within

Are the thoughts feelings imaginings of
several different women

I think that I can feel as another woman
would

I think I can do what some other women could

I think that I'm grateful I am a woman and not a man

Because that means what it does, was that part of the plan

Whether you are from here or there

Allow your dwelling place to be imbued with care

It doesn't matter so much where you come from

But, do you know the difference between 'stupid' and 'dumb'

Can you love someone as they are

Or do you try to change them as you
would steal a car

Can you be accepting and not agree

Or does it always come at a fee

Let all the things you do be kind, lead by
your heart

And if you are of color, in the U. S., be
a woman full of 'African American Art'




The End

www.ingramcontent.com/pod-product-compliance
Lightning Source LLC
Chambersburg PA
CBHW081600170526
45166CB00009B/2768